BYKER

To
Happy Birthday
Love Paul

BYKER

Sirkka-Liisa Konttinen

BLOODAXE BOOKS

in association with

AMBERSIDE

To the people of Byker

Second impression published 1988 by
Bloodaxe Books Ltd,
P.O. Box 1SN,
Newcastle upon Tyne NE99 1SN,
in association with
Amber/Side, 5 & 9 Side,
Newcastle upon Tyne NE1 3JE.

First impression published 1985 by
Bloodaxe Books Ltd
in association with The Bookhouse.

First published in Great Britain by
Jonathan Cape Ltd in 1983.

ISBN: 0 906427 90 8

Bloodaxe Books Ltd acknowledges
the financial assistance of Northern Arts.

British Library Cataloguing in Publication Data

Konttinen, Sirkka-Liisa
    Byker.
    1. Byker (Tyne & Wear (Metropolitan County))
    ——History——Pictorial works
    1. Title
    942.8′76   DA690.B/

Printed in Great Britain by
Balding + Mansell Limited, Wisbech, Cambridgeshire.

Introduction

Standing on top of Byker Hill, John Wesley exclaimed of the breath-taking panorama beneath his feet: 'A vision of Paradise!' Presumably, in 1790, it actually excluded Byker, since Byker then was a village, and mostly behind his back. His vision of Paradise was the city of Newcastle down in the valley.

The small green village surrounded by farms became an industrial suburb surrounded by shipyards, engine works, potteries and glassworks. By 1911 Byker housed some 50,000 people; a strong, self-contained community of artisans servicing a booming local industry. Situated on the north bank of the river Tyne and east of the centre of the city its proud new streets ran down in a grid-iron pattern towards the river and the city.

For me, in 1970, the vision began from the hill, sweeping down along the steep cobbled streets with row upon row of terraced flats, into the town, over the river and the bridges and beyond. The streets of Byker, serene in the morning sun with smoking chimney pots, offered me no Paradise; but I was looking for a home.

Walking down Janet Street on that soft Saturday morning in the late autumn, I was put under a spell. That spell was to last for ten years; after which there were no women to stand in the doorways and no dogs to doze on the pavements, and no streets to run down the steep hill.

Unhurried Saturday shoppers in Raby Street. Bursts of merriment outside the grocer's shop and in the butcher's queue. The baker's tray cooling off by the door, beside the bacon and the buns. Frankie Laine reaching out to a passing audience from a wind-up gramophone outside Henry's Square Deal Store: 'East is East and West is West, and never the twain shall meet', and then, with the same resounding confidence: 'Love is a Golden Ring...'

Three weeks later I was pushing around my first proud possession in my own little upstairs flat in Mason Street. Once satisfied I had found it a place, I wound it up, threw open its volume-control doors, and let loose 'Sparrow in the Treetop' – to bounce around the tiny room, and to welcome me home.

I came from a small papermill town in Finland via a short stay at Helsinki University, and a film school in London. Out to acquire skills on a meagre bankloan, and to learn about life.

An obstinate dreamer, I was anxious that Life was passing me by – out there at the travelling fair, where the hypnotist's daughter, dark and mysterious, lay in rigid suspense on the tip of a ten foot pole ... I longed to leave the commonplace.

So I arrived – from one set of conventions to another; a stranger in more than one sense.

'She's left home' (neglecting her duty towards her parents). 'She comes from Finland, such a beautiful place, nice and clean, and she *chooses* to live in Byker' (what's the matter with her?). And a year later. 'She hasn't got her nets up *yet*. She plays the *piano*; she drives a *van* (thundering scrapheap, never seen a bucket of water), *and* rides a rusty bicycle (she rides anything, her!). She goes round taking photographs, and *gives* them away for nowt (she working for the S.S., or just a mug?). And she doesn't cotton on to half the cracks, poor soul – mind, A cannot understand a word of what she says either. But she's all right – canny, aye. Poor little bairn, so far from home, and is she even married to that man?'

The first night I sat alone in the 'Hare and Hounds' I was taken under the collective wing. The drinks arrived with but a smile and a nod from an assortment of kindly faces round the room.

Mrs Dunn tucked me to her bosom (she already cared for thirteen children of her own, and managed many waifs and strays). 'That man of yours, does he belt ye? – You come and tell old Mrs Dunn – number seventeen – if he so much as lifts a finger against you hinny, and I shall see to him!' She patted my hand, and for a moment I wasn't a perfect alien.

A week later I saw her in the street again. She linked my arm, winked and steered me to the pawnshop. 'He's a fine young man, your man', she beamed at me, 'bless you both', and she pressed a piece of folded paper into my hand, with a wedding ring inside. I wore that ring, for her, till it dropped off my finger, and speeding down the pavement finally bounced out of sight, and out of my life.

I made another friend: a silky haired cheeky tom, sneakily seduced by saucerfuls of creamy milk. He moved in from next door, when it came to a choice between me and an Alsatian puppy, and made my house his abode. I still remember his pert little face in my backdoor window, and his inspired darting under my Sunday papers. He vanished one day, like all the other cats in my street, and I was united with the neighbourhood in shameless speculation. My house – and the little lad who kept pigeons in the backlane – were never to be the same again.

I was working as a founder member of Amber Associates, a group of film-makers and photographers who were struggling to establish a creative relationship with working-class communities in the North East. While piecing together a living from freelance and educational work, I started to photograph Byker in earnest. I roamed around the streets by day and hung about by night: chasing my heartbeats, stumbling in and out of other people's lives; striving to share my excitement through photographs where words would fail me. This was the beginning of my great adventure.

I received a grant from Northern Arts to set up a portrait studio in an empty hairdressing salon in Raby Street, and invited passers-by for a free photograph. The studio, with a beautifully hand painted sign 'Sair Fyeld Hinny' (title of a Northumbrian song about the sadness of getting old), was raided by scrapmen, past recovery, and boarded up.

I moved on to photograph families at home. It grew to be my ambition to photograph every household in my street.

I knocked on all the doors, explaining my mission.

'I'm sorry pet, but I've never had a photo took of me in all me life. It's nee good now, hinny, I'm past it now.'

'Well, hinny, I've got hundreds of pictures, I don't need another one took. Come and see for yerself; got so many I don't know what to do . . .'

'Me husband works night shift . . . no, I can't be bothered, pet, but thanks all the same.'

I got a yes from half the households, and half of those had better things to do when I turned up with the equipment. But I did manage to capture a fine series of mantelpiece displays, which were always promptly made available for my documentation. Lovingly arranged, in perfect symmetry, they were meant for the admiring visitor.

My work in Byker became known, accepted and assisted, and my collection of photographs, poems, reminiscences and memories began to grow.

Being a foreigner gave me one advantage: I could be nosy, and be forgiven. Many doors were opened for me that would possibly have remained closed to another photographer, and invitations extended to the kind of hospitality and intimacy that would normally be reserved for family only.

An oddball, I was hurled into a peculiar net of relationships; shortcutting into friendship and unquestioned loyalty while pining to be a native on equal ground. Adopted again and again with undeserved generosity, yet remaining outside, and not belonging. My relationships in the community grew and fumbled, got tender, tangled, and eventually established.

The studio attracted many visitors, some returning daily with new stories and old photographs. Among them was a faith-healer, who 'spoke in tongues' – a woman of commendable power and perception. Having lost a daughter, she became unduly devoted to me, and maintained a close contact with me for our remaining years in Byker. She always predicted my troubles and thoughts before setting foot in the shop, but never attempted to practise on me as I had no faith. I saw her heal her many patients, and one day she took me to her house to show me concrete proof of her gift: a myriad of multi-coloured pills, prescribed for her own fatal illness and stored away in boxes as she healed herself through God. She said she always prayed for me.

I first met Willie playing a mouth organ at a street wedding. He had popped the wee instrument into his mouth, to free his hands for the spoons, and he danced like a nimble circus bear. He later polished off his act by including a hat trick and an anecdote or two, and he often entertained all day in Isaac's second hand shop. As a young man he worked in the Royal Victoria Infirmary, and in a boiler room explosion lost acres of skin. He was dipped in ether, rolled into cotton wool and left to hang on, whereby he survived to tell one tall story after another.

He used to turn up in my studio with a plastic parrot, and a fiddle with Guarneri rubber-stamped on the inside – a fine instrument, which he couldn't play but loved to be photographed with. He was a champion draughts player; and was capable of standing in an immaculately frozen pose for a quarter of an hour at a time, as he frequently failed to plug in his hearing aid for further instructions.

His unconnected hearing aid was used to many evil ends; I once watched in awe a Jehovah's Witness overcome with confusion, as Willie, a devout Catholic, set about to put her right on the holy scriptures. She never stood a chance, and finally, utterly demoralized, withdrew her foot from the door.

Willie's sister, much to her brother's disapproval, enjoyed an occasional drink, and kicked up a leg to prove it. She was habitually to be found in the 'Hare and Hounds', where she told my fortune each time we met. I took it as a compliment that it was *such* a fortune; the make of the car and other minor details changed from time to time, but I was clearly to be fabulously rich with my photographic business ('if only she would start charging for her photographs!'). But she worried a friend of mine out of her mind with her portentous summary of her character and marital tangles, after only a few moments of unembarrassed observation in the pub.

The 'Hare and Hounds' became my local, being at the bottom of my street. Mothers, daughters and grand-daughters gathered together in the evening for a chat and a song, and duels were fought between old lovers across the room.

'Sweethearts will never grow old, as we grow old together. I'll always love you as you are today, I'll always love you the same old way . . .'

And from the other side of the room in an equally quaking voice:

'How long it is since she washed horsel, Aa really divven knaa. She's gorra face just like a spiced cake, an' as black as any cra . . .'

Sweet Lily, going eighty, and nifty at dominoes (till they were banned after a lunchtime brawl in the backroom) had an impressive high-pitched voice with much-admired quivering glissandos. Her nightly performances came to a sudden end one icy morning as she slipped off the pavement and broke an ankle.

We got her a clapped-out wheelchair from Miller's Auction Rooms, and began to wheel her to the pub of a night time. She enjoyed the rides so much her friends started hinting she'll never walk again. After six weeks I gave up with the wheeling and she got up.

She never forgot or forgave.

I made – and lost – younger friends too. A teenage couple, newly married and much in love, asked for a photo-graph of me as they left the street to join the army. As

7

a special token she had dyed her lovely long hair blonde to look like mine, and they sang for me their last night in the pub. I never saw them again, except in his mother's photographs.

The demolition gnawed around the corner; e/o (electricity off) occasionally daubed into f/off, as door after door received the stamp of death. Bricked up, deaf and dumb façades of empty streets invited fleeting dark thoughts: I wonder if they all got out.

The thirteen-year-olds in Byker were into Aggro. The rumoured big night of a ritual showdown never took place on the bonfire field; the Welbeck crew retreated without a clash. The superiority channelled itself into song:

Skinheads, weeheads, smoothies, too
Come and join our Byker crew
Byker crew are hard and smart ones
Kick you up the arse with Doctor Martin's.
If you come to our estate
Give you bovver with the aggro feet.
If you want to join our ranks
You've got to have the ability of Gordon Banks.
In the olden times men were men
There were no hairy bastards then . . . etc.

In spite of their noisy bravado they were genuine kids, highly spirited; and frequently in trouble. I now see them pushing their own babies in the street; smartly dressed, married, divorced . . . unemployed; their time of rebellion and adventure so short-lived, so long ago.

My photographs began to appear in my photographs. Framed on walls, standing on mantelpieces, carried in wallets – sent overseas.

The demolition was catching up with Byker. The countdown on streets and houses and friends began; the melancholia set in.

The wash-house closed down, and many months after the merry celebration and dancing and singing the women who toiled and gossiped and laughed together in the steam and the noise, sat lost and lonely in the coin-operated launderettes beyond the main street, complaining about the price and the inefficiency of the machines.

The pork butcher moved to North Shields to start a new business; the cobbler retired and left for Canada to join his daughter.

Mrs Potter, born, wed and widowed in a street as old as herself kindly closed her door on the man who came to sell her a wonderful future elsewhere.

'Thank you, hinny, but I belong here.'

Mr and Mrs McCartney sat amongst their packed-up orange boxes in an empty house for a year and a half waiting to be moved.

'We'll be sitting here till the day we die.'

Death and demolition clung together in the collective consciousness. Mrs Johnson, with husband ill and out of work, feared it catching up with her children. She put it in a poem:

Children among filth and grime
pass away their leisure time
with bleeding hands from throwing stones,
cut feet and broken bones.
Some poor lambs I fret to say
never lived to move away.

The conversation in the street skated around: Who's going, where, when. Who died only a week after moving. Who never saw a new house at all.

'It's wicked,' said Mr Burness, collecting his wife's brasses off the wall. 'These houses have been under demolition order for twenty odd year, and you know – they could've been saved . . . They could've just given us a bath and hot water.'

When my house finally came down with a clean sweep of the swinging ball, I stood and watched gulping at a distance.

From that moment I began to miss my downstairs neighbour who sent the Incredible Hulk to raise hell about my antique hoover interfering with her telly; who patiently stood on her doorstep clocking in and out my friends; who directed visitors to my house saying: 'It's the only dirty step in the street, you can't miss it.' (I somehow never got round to cleaning the windows, and just as well, as I didn't have any nets, but the step was a matter of principle.)

One way or another I had grown to be a part of my street, and the community. It had been my first own home, and a real home for me.

As my neighbour Nancy points out proudly: 'When she first came in our street, she couldn't tell hello from tarra, and now she speaks *Finnish* with a Geordie accent.' I had come a long way.

My final, and most treasured, compliment arrived in the post, months after I had moved away. It read: 'Not only did you immortalize Byker, and its many famous characters – You were one of them.'

13

'There was eight of us, wasn't there, or nine?
I don't remember how many there were of us,
we were like bloody rats. There was Lucy, Billy,
me, Jackie, Jenny, Tommy, Arthur, Albert,
Dawn, Annie . . . that's eleven. And me mother
had twins that died, well that makes fourteen.
And for all wor dad had a cobbler's shop I never
had a pair of shoes when I was a kid.

'I remember there was one day me father told
me to go to a grocery store on Shields Road
to get two pennworth of bacon pieces. It was
freezing cold; eight o'clock in the morning and
I was waiting outside the shop, for the shop
to open at eight thirty; I had to go to school
for nine. I was standing on me hands – no shoes,
for all we had a cobbler's shop, no shoes on
me feet. A gentleman came up and he says: "Got
no shoes, sonny?" A says: "No," he says:
"Come with me." He took us across the road
to a shoeshop and bought us a pair of shoes!
He tries them on us in the shop, A had no
stockings. "Ooh," A says, first pair on you know,
"yes, they are lovely!" But the buggers were
tight as a drum. "Ooh," A says, "they are
smashing!" I was frightened in case he took them
off us again, you see.

'So there's me with the bacon and the box
and the shoes, and me dad says: "Where did
ye get those?!" A says: "A gentleman bought
them for us on Shields Road!" Proud as Punch,
me first pair of shoes . . . Well they were that
tight I couldn't get them off! Me dad pulled
them off and gave them to a younger brother.'

18

'Me aunt Harriet Taylor had twenty-two children and a lodger. She lived above Shepherds ragshop down Byker Bank, and she only had the one big room. Alive with rats it was, and they all had to sleep and live in it.

'There was one day she was lying in bed having this bairn, and there's two lying in coffins waiting to be carried out. She used to get them to a certain age, and then they would die . . . well, she run out of names, there was three called Harry.

'She was the kindest of women. She had no money 'cause her man used to drink a lot and wouldn't tip up. But every Sunday you went out she would have a ha'penny lined on the mantelpiece for you . . . very kind she was.'

25

'I had my second baby the summer after the war. It was a very hot summer. He was a big hefty baby, eight and a half pound. I had him at home – in those days you did.

'There was something the matter with the baby. He never stopped crying; so I took him to the doctor, and he says: "The trouble with you women, you always think there's something wrong with a baby that cries, take him home he's fine." The baby cried the whole time we were at the surgery. I took him to the same doctor three times in all.

'August the fourth – he was born July the fourth – he slept the whole night, and for the first time he didn't cry. I picked him out of his cot in the morning – he was blue, he was dead! I run down the stairs crying with him on me arms, and me mum shouting: "Put him back in the cot!" 'Cause she was old fashioned, she thought I would get into trouble.

'It was my twentieth birthday a fortnight before. Oh, it was terrible . . . terrible. The doctor came – the same one – and this Scottish woman who lived in our house, she gave him a right mouthful, but he didn't care. Later on he said he'd never seen the baby before, but his bill arrived all right: fifteen shillings. Five shillings a time you had to pay if you didn't belong to a club.

'I was told there would have to be a post mortem. The baby was took away and a funeral was arranged for the Saturday. You had a proper funeral when a baby was a month old, it wasn't just put down in some corner of a churchyard. All the women had bought us flowers, everybody was there – and then they telld us they hadn't done the post mortem yet. That was the worst part of it. I had to spend the whole weekend in a house full of wreaths – he was buried on the Monday.

'A proper little grave. I used to go and visit it, but I could hear him cry, so I stopped going. It's a terrible thing when your baby dies. You never forget it for the rest of your life.'

'That's Stephen, my grandson. His mother went away fifteen year ago, and left him in a backlane. She come in our house on a Saturday and she says: "Stephen, I'm going for your birthday card." "Can I come with ye, can I come with ye?!" She says: "Oh, I'm just taking Peter and Davy," but never mind, she took him and all. They went in this shop, and left him looking at a donkey in a backlane outside. Of course, eventually, he come round here: "Is me ma here?" "Well," A says, "you should know where your ma is, you went out with her!" He says: "Aye, but she said she was going for me card!"

'It was there on the table when we went in. Her man – that's my son – goes long distance lorry driving, he's away. A thought, oh natural, you know what A mean, and me husband says: "She'll come when she's ready." Monday, no sign of her. Come Wednesday, A says: "There's something wrong. Them two bairns have never been away as long as this."

'We never found her or the two bairns. That was fifteen years ago. Stephen was seven and a half when she left him. I brought him up the best I could, but it left him feeling inferior, you know what A mean. At school he'd cry, cry, cry. A told the doctor, A says: "Why is he crying? I do all I can for him, I'm giving him things I never give me own sons." He says it's his mother leaving him.

'Well, poor soul, it took him many, many years before he could mix with the world. One day, he was about seventeen, he come in and he says: "Mother, I've got a job!" A says: "Where son?!" He says: "I'm a bouncer!" A says: "A bouncer?! In a night club?!" A says, "Son, anybody just looks at you makes you cry!"

'But I say it's made him the man he is today.'

29

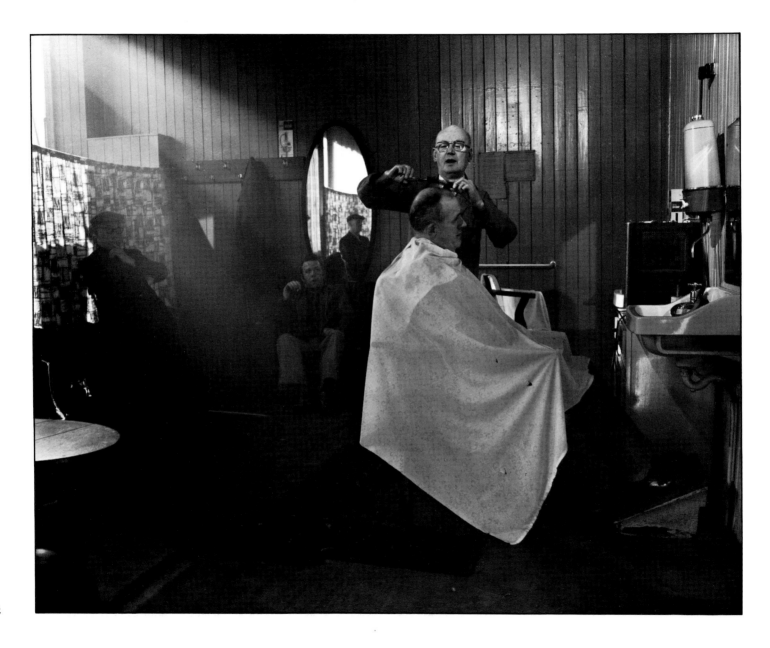

32

'You notice I took a pair of shoes off you, and I didn't have to put your name on them or anything. I mean I put the names on practically all the shoes, but if I didn't know your name it wouldn't matter. I can remember anyway. You see every time I handle a pair of shoes I picture the person they belong to. Like when I take them off the shelf and put them on the machine A says to meself: "Oh aye. That's the lovely young lass with a dog, Mrs Fairbairn." Or: "That's the wife with a moustache." Or: "That's old Billy the chimneysweep from Carville Road." Every time I pick up a pair I remember who it belongs to. When I've finished with them I enter them in a book, so that if some-body comes in and says: "I've just had them shoes heeled last week," I can refer to the book and say: "You didn't have them heeled last week, you had them heeled last Christmas!" I also put a mark on me shoes, a nail in a cer-tain position, so as when somebody comes in and says: "I had these shoes done here last week," I can check them and say: "What a terrible job, hinny, but they weren't done by me!"'

'Monday was a washday; it was who will get the line oot first! Ye might go to the wash-hoose, but if ye weren't rich ye had to be quick, 'cause the wash-hoose was thru'pence an hour! Why yes. Everybody was doing their washing, and you could hear the gramophones in the back yards. On Tuesday ye did yer rooms, Wednesday the front stairs. Thursday was yer blacklead day. Friday ye did yer brasses and door-knobs and Saturday yer scullery. Aye. Ye cleaned yer double decker fender on a Monday, wrapped it up and put it doon again on a Friday, shining like a shilling. And every night before ye went oot courting ye had to do a square of yer mother's clippy mat; she always had one in a frame. But on a Sunday ye weren't to wash a pair of stockings, oh no, Sunday was a Sabbath day. If ye attempted, yer mother would say ye'll go the moon, and ye had that much put into yer head ye thought she was right. But the war changed that; ye had to work on a Sunday.'

'We didn't have it as hard as some. Me mother was working you see. She used to make a big suet pudding, a great big'n, and say: "Them that eats the most pudding gets the meat!" Everybody dived in, and of course by the time ye finished the pudding ye had nee room for the meat, ye didn't want it. Ye mothers were crafty in them days, weren't they Jenny. I knew a woman, she had a Jew come round once a week for a sixpence, used to sell frocks for little girls. If she hadn't the sixpence she would tie her door knocker up and put a note on the door: Please do not knock, husband very ill! – Hello Georgina!
'But ye didn't hear anybody complaining, did ye Jenny. If ye went short ye run to the pawnshop with a pair of sheets or a suit, and if ye mother couldn't afford to get your suit oot on the Friday, ye stopped in till the next Friday. Here's me friend Bella.
'Hello, Bella pet!
'Bella and me speak such broad Geordie that we sometimes don't understand each other, do we Bella?'

'*A naa, but A can talk polite when A gan oot ye naa.*'

'A naa ye can Bella A naa. Tara love.

'A had a friend – her father owned a bicycle shop in Walls-end – she married this lad, a lovely lad. They didn't want him to have her 'cause he wasn't high enough up for her, but never mind, she married him. – This is God's truth; she sent her mam a piece of her wedding cake and her mam put it through a mangle and sent it back! – But she got married, and her man hardly ever worked. There was one time her bairn took pneumonia and before she could send for the doc-tor she had to take the sheets off her bed, run to the wash-hoose with them and run to the pawnshop for to get the doc-tor's fee. The old Mr Glendenning examined the sheets; he says: "These feel a bit damp Mrs Armstrong." She says: "Oh, it's the hoose Mr Glendenning, it's dreadful damp wor hoose!" From washing them in such a hurry you see. And as the doctor come up the front stairs to see her child he has his hand oot for the money.

'But I would still say they were happier times in many ways. There wasn't as much crime. You hardly ever heard of a murder, ye weren't frightened to walk in the street. Aye. People were friendlier. 'Course they had to be. Ye never knew when ye had to go to the woman next door for to come and give you a hand 'cause ye were in the family way, the bairn was coming. But now ye don't care if yer neighbour looks at ye. She might have fifty watches and she'll not give you the time – 'cause you've probably got two an' all.'

'A deen't knaa how he wandered off to the railway line.'

'*Could've just been standin' on the platform, and the draught of a passing train pulled him in.*'

'Aye. Could've been that.'

'*He was quite hefty though.*'

'Noo. He wasn't that heavy, Agnes. In fact he looked fatter than he was. The coat made him look fatter an' all. 'Course he's been oot of fettle lately. Been havin' fits an' that.'

'*Oh, has he?!*'

'Too finely bred, that was his trouble.'

'*What was that you say, Lily?*'

'He was too finely bred!'

'*Finely bred, aye; that's the trouble. A wouldn't have a pedigree for a pet.*'

44

'You can be too soft, can't you. Like our Dorothy.

'A gans to see her one day, she's hoovering in the scullery, you know. "Mam, he hasn't been home since yesterday." A says: "Go up to the depot and see what time he finished work!" So she goes up.

' "What time did Mr Chapman finish work yesterday?" The man says: "He wasn't at work yesterday." "But he was – he went out with his uniform on!" He says: "He might have went out with his uniform, but he resigned on Thursday." "What!!?" He says: "Did you not know?" She says: "No, and I'm his wife!" She comes down and says: "He's packed his job up!" "Eeh, well," A says, "you've better gan and report him missing." Because he could've been in the hospital or many a thing. So A gans down for to put it in the paper.

'It was well planned. He'd had the car ready at the door to take his case, and he says to our Neil: "There's eight pence, go and get some sweets." 'Cause if his bairn had seen him with his case he would've wanted to know where he was gannin' you see.

'Well never mind – A'm ganning down to the *Evening Chronicle* on Raby Street. A sees this wife, she says: "Where you gannin', Ruby?" A says: "Doon the paper to report our Dolly's man's missing." Six o'clock there's a knock on me door. "Ruby, A've got something to tell you – your Dorothy's man's done off with a conductress." "Eeh," A says, "A daren't tell our Dolly, better let her find out for herself."

'So here . . . she says: "Mother, will you come to the depot with me to see how much he had to pick up?" We were on the bus – I was always well known on the buses; 'cause they used to say: "Is Ruby on, divven't set the bus away till she's on" – so A says to the conductor: "What do you think of Mr Chapman?" "Him, the turd," he says, "they tell me he's left a canny bit lass and two bairns." But he says, the one he's away with, ooh, she's not worth a light! Married with a bairn she went away with a married man with eight bairns – her man took her back – then she went

47

away with a young lad that was engaged, and her man took her back – but this time she's supposed to have a bairn to our Dolly's man. It's supposed to be his, but it'll be somebody else's like.

'So we gans to the depot to ask how much he'd picked up. Twenty four pound. She says to the fella: "Twenty four pounds! You know how much he left me?! Three!" "Your husband was in such a state," he says. "My husband was in such a state! How do you think I feel after being married fourteen year, and no note nor nothing!?"

'So, of course, on the Tuesday – she gets a letter from him.

' "Dear Dorothy, you know by now I have left you. Our marriage has been a shambles; we haven't had time to sit down and talk. I love and miss my children. Maybe some day they will forgive me, I know you never will. When I get myself settled down I shall see you all right financially." She never had a halfpenny off him.

'But she got a divorce. She's working at the British Home Stores, well, she's got to. And to look at him you think butter wouldn't melt in his bloody mouth.

'You can be too soft, can't you.

'He used to stop out all night. "I've been to me friends – A got too drunk," A says to Dolly: "You're like a pawnshop, you take owt in."

'There was one day our Neil come doon. A says: "Is your da at work?" "No," he says, "he's been out all night." "Out all night!" A says to meself I'll take a walk up. There she is hoovering around. "They tell me Fred's been out all night." She says: "How do you know?" – "Birds fly."

'So in he comes. He has to start work at half past one, it's one o'clock. She says: "Where have you been?" He says: "I was at a party, I was that drunk I missed me bus." A says: "You could've got the bloody train!" She goes out into the scullery, and I hear her say: "tarrah, tarrah . . ." So when she come in A says: "He's been to a knocking shop!" She says: "Eeh, what do you mean! Fancy talking like that!" A

says: "I'm older than you, I know. No married man is going to stop out of his house for nowt."

'He'd been ganning with Her, you see. Nowt, nowt to look at – she looks exactly what she is – a little cow. Naturally she knew our Fred was a married man. She used to phone to the wife upstairs for him. Well, A blame her, Mrs Green, 'cause if she'd been any sort of a woman at all, she would've said to our Dolly: "Dolly, come up, there's a wife on the phone, wants to speak to your Fred – you watch for it." You know. Her husband saw Fred in the bar and he says: "Fred, you are our friend, and Dolly's our friend – I don't want you to have your love-line on my phone." "Oh," he says, "it won't happen again."

'I was there at the divorce hearing. Me and me friend went – our Dolly wouldn't. As we were going up the stairs there's Him with two lasses and a solicitor. He turns around and says: "Oh, here comes the mother." As I pass him he brushes his hair with his hand, casually, to show off a ring on his finger – She must have bought it for him. Me friend thought A was gonna barge in, so she says: "Howay Ruby, you've seen him!" A says: "It's not him I want to see, it's his little fancy bit." There was two of them and A couldn't tell which was which. It wasn't long they shouted: "Chapman versus Chapman!" Him and Her comes down, he's got his arm around her. I'm sitting in the corner, watching them ganning doon. He opens the door for her, and I pounces on the pair of them and shouts: "Yous two right bloody shithouses, yous will get your day!!" Not a murmur – straight oot the door.

'Our Dolly's never seen him since he left her, twenty year ago. You wonder . . . She used to believe everything he said, and she used to think he would come back one day. She would put out his slippers beside the fire.

'Between me and you I think she would have him back.'

H stands for happiness, and happiness to you!
O stands for old folks ever true
M stands for mother, you'll find there is no other, no matter where you roam
E stands for everyone and everyone loves HOME

52

'My husband is paralysed down one side. He took a slight stroke when he was shaving on a Thursday and cut his face all over – you never saw such a mess. The doctor said he hadn't to shave, his whiskers would have to grow. What a mess he was, eeh. I washed his face every day with carbolic soap and hot water till the cuts healed up. I'm having an awful job shaving him. He's got a big dimple on his chin, and his mouth's twitching all the time. There's one or two small scars and I'm still knocking them off. I keep saying: "Eeh, Johnny, I've knocked them spots off again!" and he says: "Oh, go on Betty, you are doing your best, you are doing your best." '

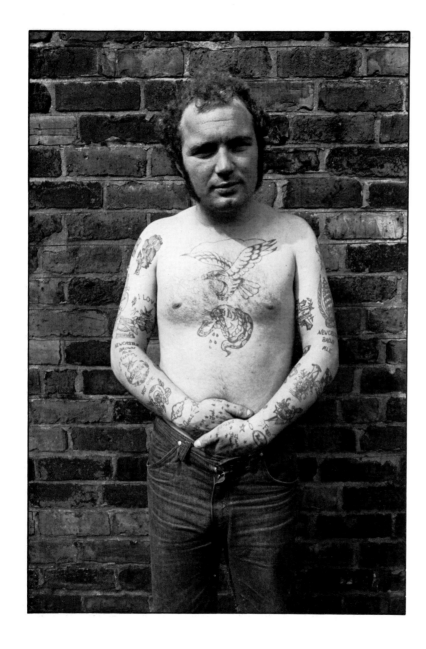

'Oh aye, not a bad photo, just a bit dark. Well, ye cannot see the inside of the shop! It's the shop that's coming doon, not me ye bugger. A'm planning to stay in the trade, mind A hope A find an easier job than this. Do ye want a bit sausage for yer dinner? A bet ye neva had a bit better sausage than this, what ye say Maggie?'

'*No, it's lovely. (A say owt, man.)*'

'She'll be coming back saying: "Keep me a bit o' that sausage for Christmas." '

'*Can A see yer photo? Eeh, lovely – nice and clear. Flatters ye, mind! Wor Sandra's got one of them coloured cameras. Have ye got a photo of me in yer box?*'

'God, she's got a million.'

'*Lovely. Let's have a look.*'

'What a lovely photo!'

'That's you there, flower.'

'That's not me!'

'That's you.'

'What a horrible photo!'

'You just said ye liked it!'

'I like the photo. Aye, it'll be me the more I look at it. I always sit on the same seat, the third one on the end.'

'Of course it's you, ye daft bat.'

'Well it looks like me with all the rings on me fingers. A won twenty poond eighty on Monday night! I gave him seven poond. A have to give him a third every time, you know! Mind, he'll do the same for me, but he never wins. It's always me forking out the money.'

'Make the tea pet, will ye.'

'Can't make the tea till it boils.'

'Boiling.'

'Catched two vandals in the next yard yesterday. They had a dustbin full of lead piping, they'd left the water flying!! A goes in the yard – they were pulling the sink units out – A says: "What the hell are ye doing like?!" (You have to be rough, let them know ye are not frightened.) A says: "You've been up at that window!" The little fat one says: "We are from the Gasboard." A says: "Divven't ye come that wi' me, ye are from the Gasboard! The Gasboard man's just locked that bottom door!" That woman wasn't ten minutes oot of her hoose! If A had a gun A would've bloody shot them!'

'Get your soup!'

'A hit ye in the eye the minute ye talk to me like that!'

'A says get your soup, that's all. It's getting cold.'

'He's a waster an all, lad next door. He's been stealing the copper wire that's been burned from our telly, he says he can get money for it.'

'Seven poond.'

'Seven poond! He'll put it doon his neck wi' beer. His wife's left him wi' two bairns. A don't blame her, he wants leaving.'

'I see he's cooking chips for his bairns today. A'm enjoying me dinner an' all. You see we have our dinner on a Sunday, and what's left we have the bugger warmed up on a Monday and we still enjoy it! Of course A get nowt to eat for the rest of the week.'

'He's supposed to be on a diet for sugar. Sugar wants to come oot of the top of his heed! One minute he's with it, the next minute he's not, so as soon as he knows he's not, away he goes to his belly. A just let him gan on.'

'I've enjoyed that the day as what A did yesterday. I always tell her when I enjoy it, and I tell her when it's rotten an' all, and I get wronged.'

' 'Cause it's never rotten! As ill as A was yesterday you got a beautiful dinner. Mind, A went on the bed after that. Never get married pet, it's not worth it.'

'Not a finer thing in your life. Especially when you get married a fourth time.'

'He's married three. A wouldn't put it past him – if I was gone tomorrow he'd have another wife. But he'd have to have a better place to fetch her in.'

'We'll be going to Tom Collins House, you know, for old folks. What a lovely place! You ring a bell for a nurse – two rings if ye want a young one! You get a free fridge and an electric cooker and it costs you a shilling a year for yer telly!'

' "You'll be the first out of Kendal Street," the man said. They've never bothered their backsides aboot us since. We've had our stuff packed a year gone Christmas.'

'*A think we'll be dead before we shift.*'

'A've tellt them to bring the bulldozer up, and I'll lie doon and let them squash me. I'm not worried, I'm past worrying. It's got me so upset I cannot eat.'

'*Want some furniture, pet? Divven't knaa what to do with it. The antique man come to view your houses you know. "Ooh", he says, "hinny – you are all modern!!" But as you can see pet, the only thing that's modern in this house is me, and I'm getting on.*'

'Everybody pawned.

'I remember one time I was very hard up. I was only youngly married, and me husband was on the Parish. I goes up Chillingham Road, and I sees this big jumble sale for tuppence. Well, I picked up some nice baby's things and a pair of troosers, got the whole lot for one and ten. Come back, got the iron out and put it on the fire. Cleaned the things, pressed them up and run to the pawnshop. I got eight and sixpence. When I came out, I met this wife in the street. "I see you've been to the pawnshop Sally." "Aye." "Do ye ever get nice pawn tickets to sell?" "Why, I've just pawned a smashing pair of men's troosers and some lovely little lasses' things." "Eeh," she says, "do ye want much for the ticket?" A says: "Why no, you can have it for three bob." You see! Eight and six and three bob I selld the ticket for. When I come home me mother says: "What have you done wor Sara?!" "Oh," A says, "divven't worry yoursel mother, I haven't pinched it!" "Eeh, my God," she says, "have ye met somebody better off than yoursel?" I telld her, and she says: "Lord be praised, for to help the poor people!"

'The wife downstairs, she had a family of twelve, and on a Monday morning she used to take all her suits to the pawn-shop for to pay her rent and to buy some food. On the Friday night when she got her pay she went and got them oot again. It was tuppence to have them on a hanger or penny on the shelf. Well the best part of yer mothers wouldn't pay tup-pence to have them on a hanger, so on the Saturday ye could spot in the street all the suits from the shelves, 'cause they all had pawnshop folds. And on the Monday they went back in the pawnshop for the landlord.

'I knew a woman used to pawn her husband's razor for nine pence and get it out again for ten pence. Twice a week she'd take it out, run home with it and run back again the same day after he had his shave.'

'When I win the pools I will move to Cresswell and buy
a bungalow and get a cabin cruiser and go fishing.'

'I had a pigeon once that won a lot of money, and it only had one eye. For me, there's some atmospherics in the air that guides the pigeon, 'cause when you get a thundery weather, the pigeons, ooh, they're lost, they divven knaa where the' are . .

'The scientists, they cannot tell you. It's got them puzzled.'

'A think pigeons, they have a photographic eye. They must take a print of the place, eh, because looka when pigeons is flying, say from London, look at all them gardens, rooftops, all the same as what the' got here, aren't the', and yet the' pass over all them roofs, little plots of grass, and come right back to this little place, so what do ye think of that, hinny? A think it's marvellous. To me, pigeons are fascinating. A've been among them for fifty-seven year.

'They reckon pigeon men are a bit daft. Why, we never even go for a holiday. Even as a kiddie I was always interested in birds, such as a little sparrow. When I left school A says to meself I'm going to have pigeons, A'm going to race them. So that's what I did. And now, I never leave the garden now, except when A go for me dinner. It's not that I want to win a lot of money or owt like that. I just like to watch their antics; they are like human beings really, I like to sit here and watch them. There was one here, ooh, what a queer one. When I let him out he would go wandering about on his own, and if you were talking to somebody you could bet your boots he'd be sitting there looking at you. And the way he used to turn to you when you talked to him you'd think he understood you. He didn't of course, but you know what I mean. I'm sorry I lost him, he was a real pet of mine.'

'Arthur, you told me to keep out of here.'

'*Aha.*'

'Well, if I see you over there, I'll kick your friggin' arse out of that gate!!'

'*All right, don't get yersel excited, man.*'

'I'm not excited!! I'm just telling ye aboot yer bloody cheek aboot the bloody pigeon! Now you'll have to contend with our Lenny, he'll put your last bloody tooth doon your bloody throat! He'll kill ye!!'

'*A've tellt your Lenny, Bobby's pigeon didn't stop his . . .*'

'The bloody cheek!!!'

'*I was sitting here looking at his ducket. A pigeon come over and A says to your Lenny : here's a pigeon for you, but the bird wouldn't drop. Ye cannot help them things, Joe. And ye don't go round blaming somebody else!*'

'It flew around three times!!!'

'*Right enough. You'll have Bobby to contend with when he comes in tonight.*'

'You are just a bloody mischief maker . . . looka you!!!'

'*Aha, aha.*'

'And A've tellt ye, you come inside those lofts . . .' course you'll be finished with him now, Tommy's laddy. You'll not be getting your dropsy from him now . . .'

'*I've never . . .*'

'Yes you have! You have watered his pigeons and every bloody thing. You've got your nicker off him an' all.'

'*A didn't ye knaa.*'

'You bloody well did though ye knaa!'

'*I didn't ye hear!*'

'Creepin' arse little bugger! Not the build to even fight, ye bugger.'

'*Let it drop then, Joe, let it drop.*'

'Nee bigger than a bloody pawnticket, look at ye! A'll get wor Lenny to come and sort ye oot this afternoon and God help ye!'

'*A'll be here, Joe.*'

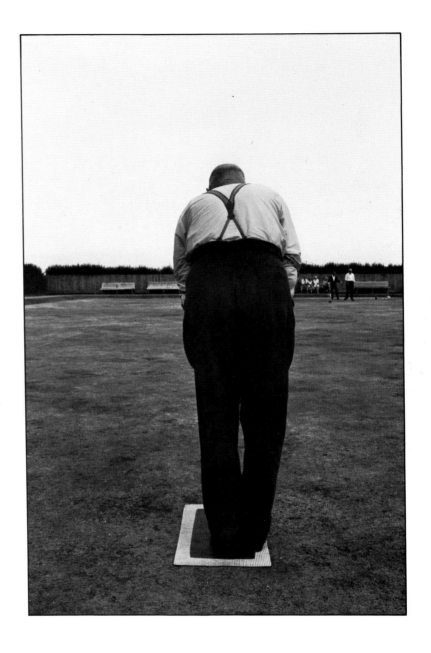

'This table is set of a night: two cups, two saucers and two plates – in case anything happens to me through the night . . . A've got it all sorted out. Our Betty, she come in and she says: "Eeh, mother, you are still setting the table!" A says: "Certainly. And now you can put the kettle on and make yourself a nice cup of tea." Well, A mean, at eighty-five you are not a young lass any more.'

'Yesterday I was here from a quarter to seven, I sat here in the backlane on sentry duty all day until pitch black at night, daren't go away. They come through the rafters and down the hatch, the buggers. I can hear them: bang, bang, bang, on all sides. A says to the police this is getting unbearable. He says: "Pack up your things, put them in boxes," but this is all we've got to look at! He says: "Take your valuables away to your son's and daughter's." So are we to go to Killingworth or Shiremoor when we want to watch our telly? A mean . . . He says: "Nail the buggers to the floor!" '

'This is God's truth. The doctor came to me mother – she looked a bit flushed and that so I got the night doctor out – he come in and he says: "She's got the flu." Well, that was bad you know, she was ninety-six, me mother. The next day he comes in and he says: "I'm afraid she's got pneumonia as well, she's very poorly." Flu and pneumonia at her age. So, of course I sent for all the family.

'This place was literally packed – sons, daughters, grand-children, great grandchildren . . . The men went out and we start to drink; we had a bottle or two in the house. And when the men come back everybody was merry. Me mother's in a coma, so me brother says: "Well, if she's dying, she's gonna go out happy," and pours some brandy down her. All of a sudden she sits up in bed and starts to sing: "Where Did You Get That Hat!"

'She's still alive, twelve month after. Mind, it took some brandy to pull her round.'

'I'm a pensioner now. I'm better off than I have ever been in me life. Same with the other pensioners here – you never hear one say they are hard up. Of course, if you want beer, you want cigarettes and Bingo, well you can't have everything.'

'Old Mr Wilson is getting buried this afternoon. That's why we are standing here, hinny. He's never been out of that hoose for fifty odd year. Aa deen't knaa whether it was just his mood or whether he's been ill or what.'

He has a daughter looked after him. It's a good job God has taken him, she's had a hard life with him, poor lass.'

'He's ninety-six you know. He had a beard doon to here!'

Aha. Eeh, he's been serious for her. He was still shouting for his tea an' that . . .'

'His sister got buried from the Wall in May, didn't she Martha. They couldn't fit the coffin into the lift, and the stairs were that narrow they had to carry her doon standing up! Fancy that, her last journey, and she still couldn't rest her poor feet!'

Aha, that's reet Aggie. They cannot lay them oot nor nowt in the new houses. Too hot. Funerals are not what they used to be.'

'No. Years ago – ooh hinny, you went to a funeral and you'd get the feed! Talk about weddings! Funerals had a far better look in!'

Why aye. And ye'd hear all the gossip . . . It was a scandalmonger place, a funeral. Ye walked all the way from the hoose to the cemetery, and they'd shut the bars and pull doon the blinds.'

'If ye were anybody like . . .'

I remember an old woman dying in our lane, Aggie. Her grand-daughter, just a little lassie then, she went round saying : "Would ye like to come and see me gran, she's dead – all the lovely trimmings, all the black ribbon . . ." And she'd charge you a ha'penny for a look! She says for to buy some flowers for the grave.'

'Eeh, what a shame! Ye cannot have a decent burial nowadays. – Nor a decent christening for that matter. A christening used to go on for three days!'

Well, they don't christen them now, Aggie. Oh, some of them don't believe in it! This'll be a land of heathens in a few more years. Ye mother wouldn't allow you over her doorstep if yer child wasn't christened, and you weren't churched!'

'And look at the way the lasses have their bairns now. You are in the hospital one day, and you're hoyed oot the next! When I had my two boys I daren't comb me hair, daren't put me hands in flour, daren't put me hands in cold water! Ye were in bed a fortnight, and ye weren't decent if ye come oot under six weeks!'

Aye. This'll be a world of heathens, I tell ye. Even the weather, just look at it! The bloomin' weather's gone all haywire! When I was a kid ye couldn't walk on the pavements on yer bare feet, they were that hot. Why aye . . .'

'I like being on me own. I've always been a loner you know, yet I don't feel lonely . . . I knit a lot and I read a lot. I go out to the shops, I go over to the club. People say: "You must be lonely." I say: "Lonely? I've got peace. Without fear."

'I used to love me Bingo. – Three years since I was in the Bingo. I liked it when my husband was alive, but I didn't like it when he died, isn't that funny. It was just to get out of the house – away from him, just for that hour. Oh, I used to love it . . .

'He had something to complain about, you know. He had asbestos in the lungs – asbestosis. He was a boilermaker in the shipyard. – A terrible disease. It grows like a tree. He couldn't breathe, it was gradually choking his lungs. Great big fella and all, never lost an ounce of weight, fresh coloured. He couldn't breathe. He used to make this noise . . . like pigeons. Nobody expected him dying mind. He was only in hospital for a day and a half.

'Vickers tried to prove he never had asbestosis. He had to wait till he was dead; they found it all right. He had a solicitor, he said we could lose everything on one small legal matter. Of course they know them things, we don't – a legal matter.

'Well he never got any compensation. That man suffered for nowt. And he wasn't the only one, there were a lot of them that died with it.

'He knew what he had. He used to read books on himself, he must have had a good heart. He says to me: "You know when you comb your hair and you put it in the sink, it goes sort of funny in the drain, it clutters, well that's my lungs." But he never thought about dying . . . He knew what he had, and he knew there was no cure, but you never heard him talk about dying – funny . . .

'He was frightened though. I couldn't get away from him, he wouldn't let me out of his sight! If I went a message, "How long will you be?" Fear is an awful thing. So that's how I used to love to get down to the Bingo – just to get out of the house, just for an hour of an afternoon. When I got back home I used to say: "Oh dear, stuck here all night again." It was watching him – suffocating – rubbing his chest . . . It must have been awful for him.

'He would never dream he'd come to depend on me as much one day. Because he was a big strong fella, and these people doesn't think anything's going to happen to them. I felt sorry for him, especially when he was in pain, but I couldn't say I felt anything else. If I ever did he soon killed it, the way he treated me.

'I was nobody you see. He knew everything. And these people knows nothing really, they just think they do. He wasn't an ignorant man, but I wouldn't say he was very intelligent either. Men in them days were domineering, especially shipyard men – they were boss. They had to have more money in their pockets than what they give you to keep the whole house and the kids, and you daren't ask for more! If you went short . . . well, you put the blame on yourself, you thought you must have been a bad manager. And sometimes you were shaking with terror, not knowing which way they were coming in . . .

'I was daft, hinny. I was brought up with a father like that and all. I didn't live in a happy house. I had a domineering father, and I got a domineering husband. So how can you wonder at me enjoying my bit peace on me own now.

'Mind you, he was the nicest lad that ever walked, when we were courting. He thought a lot of me, in his way. It was poverty that changed him. When we were going together he was working, he was a tradesman. Plenty of money in his pocket, plenty clothes. Three weeks before we were married he was laid off – he didn't work again for six years. He would say: "If I ever come to take a job, I'll take care of my money!" And by God he did.

'Mind it wasn't easy. Dole money . . . week after week, month after month, year after year, and nobody to help you because everybody was in the same boat. Eeh, we went hungry. I used to walk past the foodshops and look away, 'cause me stomach was turning over with hunger. When my last child was born, we hadn't even any maternity money. We had nothing.

'She was born on a cold February morning. The day before was Thursday, and nobody had owt to eat on a Thursday, 'cause next day you got your dole money. Well, that Thursday – ooh, I was longing for something to eat. He says: "I'll go along to me sister's, she might give us tuppence for a packet of tabs. If she does I'll do without the tabs and I'll fetch two separate penny worth of chips in. So I was lying in bed, longing for them chips. And I knew the way he walked up them stairs he hadn't gotten the tuppence. I started to cry, I couldn't help it, I was so hungry. A bairn inside you and hunger. Some people doesn't know they are born. I woke up through the night in labour. There was one penny he wouldn't part with, that was for the phone. A student doctor come. He says: "It'll be a while yet." "It's coming!! I can feel the head!" "Oh no," he says, "your waters haven't broke yet – oh my goodness!!" He jumped over the bed and brought the baby. "It's a girl, it's a girl!" he says, 'cause I had two boys jumping all over the floor. And I thought I couldn't care less. I couldn't have cared if she was dead – life was leaving me. So however, he says: "You've been a good girl, you deserve a nice cup of tea." I just looked at him, "We'll have to wait till the morning, till he goes to the dole." He says, "My God," and he put the baby in bed with me.

'Mind, God's good. He must be, 'cause he made me better. But it took a long time for me to get any strength.

'There's one thing I say for me husband. He wouldn't eat before the children did. He saw to them first; everything was shared. But that was all he did for them, he fed them . . . I had to get a job for to buy them clothes and things. – A nuisance he considered they were, he wouldn't listen to them . . . Mind you, they didn't dislike him for all that, but they knew he had never bothered with them much. Me daughter said, when she was only fourteen: "How on earth you ever married him, I don't know. What did you see about him?!" My children all think a lot of me, they know I did my best for them.

'My husband wasn't a bad man when he wasn't working . . . He'd lay down the coppers for us to plan how to use them, how to make the most of what we had. It was poverty that changed him . . . when he started work, we drifted apart. He would keep his money to himself and look back with bitterness. I used to say: "Let the past die a bit, it's gone." But he wouldn't. He'd save and save and only think of himself. And where did it get him? He's dead now, and I was left with the money after all, he never enjoyed it. Think what we could've done with it when we were still young, what pleasure it could've given us. Now I'm old and he's gone, and the money is washers anyway.'

'She was always very clean and houseproud, Emily. Even when she was bad. And she looked nice. I always complimented her when I saw her. I used to say: "Mind there's one thing about you, Emily, your hair's always in place!" I knew it was a wig like, but I didn't let on. I just admired it, 'cause it used to cheer her up.

'Poor Emily, she looked forward to the summer and a new house, but she never saw neither. She died three week ago.'

Are you lonesome tonight?
Is your brassiere too tight?
Are your corsets just drifting apart?
Are there holes in your vest
Where it touches your chest?
Is your spare tyre reaching your heart?
Are your stockings well laddered and shoes wearing thin?
Do you keep up your knickers with a safety pin?
Are your teeth old and worn?
Do they slip when you yawn?
Then no wonder you're lonesome tonight.

'What is it you're looking for, hinny, a bed or a divan?'
'*What's the difference, like?*'
'A bed's got two ends.'
'*Eeh, A deen't knaa.*'
'Let me put it this way, you are a bit more modern with a divan.'

Postscript

By 1963 the whole of Byker was scheduled for redevelopment. In that year Wilfred Burns, the then City Planning Officer in Newcastle, wrote in a book, *New Towns for Old*, that, 'In a huge city, it is a fairly common observation that the dwellers in a slum are almost a separate race of people, with different values, aspirations and ways of living,' and he went on, 'One result of slum clearance is that a considerable movement of people takes place over long distances with devastating effect on the social groupings built up over the years. But, one might argue, this is a good thing when we are dealing with people who have no initiative or civic pride. The task, surely, is to break up such groupings even though the people seem to be satisfied with their miserable environment and seem to enjoy an extrovert social life in their locality.'

Years of neglect by private landlords and prevarication by the city council had turned a once vital neighbourhood into an increasingly miserable environment for a community who did not lack either initiative or civic pride. Forced out of their homes, people in Byker expressed a firm desire to be rehoused together in the new Byker, and to have their community spirit left intact. The Conservatives selected Byker as their show-piece redevelopment project in 1968, and as a way of legitimising the council's intervention in the area, this wish was taken aboard. 'The internationally famous architect with his team of social experts around him, and supported by the council's own officials, would proceed to rebuild Byker in a way which allowed people to stay.' '. . . What the planners and architects are striving for in their multi-million pound scheme is to keep the way of life, the same faces and families together, only housed in new surroundings,' enthused one local paper, and another quoted the architect as saying: '. . . the redevelopment will be phased so that the people's desire to move from their old worn out house to a new house, down the street, as it were, will be realized.'

The plans were hailed as an example of community-based redevelopment, attracting national and international attention. In fact they proposed a significantly greater reduction of population than the forecasts which were made *before* the policy to retain the community was agreed.

The homes of 3,000 people were cleared for a motorway, which was never built. Most of the people who left Byker were given no choice about whether to stay or not, because at the time their houses were demolished there were no new ones to move into. Others would have stayed but could no longer tolerate the stress, uncertainty, dirt and decay. There has never been any attempt by the council to give them guarantees of being able to return.

Over 17,000 people lived in Byker at the start of the redevelopment. Fewer than 20 per cent of them were living in the New Byker by 1976. One is only left to speculate what would have happened had the policy *not* been to retain the community.

(These findings are derived from Peter Malpass's research on the Byker experiment in community-based redevelopment, for a study commissioned [but never published] by the Department of Environment in 1975. A full account of the Byker redevelopment story appears in his recent book, Housing Policy and Practice, *jointly written with Alan Murie, and published by Macmillan.)*

'But in them days A've been telling you about nobody was jealous of anybody. It's a different class of people in Byker now. They are never content round here. If one gets a bottle of milk, the other gets two. That's the way they go on. And they can't bear you to have anything. "So and so's got the telly, so and so's just had the phone put in, I wonder how she does it." And then if you don't go out you are mean, "make you sick, they never go out." And if you go out, "I wonder how they do it, they are never in." So what are yous to do? In the days gone by it wasn't like that – but then nobody had anything.'

The Photographs

The stories in this book, though genuine, are not about, or told by, the people in the photographs accompanying them

ACKNOWLEDGMENTS

I gratefully acknowledge the financial support of Northern Arts and Amber Associates in helping me prepare this book.

I would like to thank Peter Malpass for generously allowing me to use material based on his research on the Byker redevelopment.

I would also like to thank my friends, especially Dotty and Katrina, who assisted me on my expeditions, and the good people of Byker, who didn't mind us.   S.-L.K.